This sheet music includes 2 harp arrangements of "Castle on a Cloud" from *Les Misérables*.

Pedal harpists may play either version.

Lever harp players who tune their harps to the key of C should play the version on page 1.
You will need sharping levers on your F, C, and A strings.

Lever harp players who tune their harps to 3 flats should play the version on page 3.
You will need sharping levers on your B, E, A, and G strings.

Either version may be played on most small harps with about 26 strings if you play everything an octave higher than written. The exception is the last 2 measures. You will need to play these where they are written (instead of an octave higher), and make an additional sharping lever change for the next to the last note.

1

Castle on a Cloud
from *Les Misérables*
arrangement for lever harps tuned to C, or pedal harps

Music by Claude-Michel Schönberg
Lyrics by Alain Boublil, Jean-Marc Natel
and Herbert Kretzmer
Harp arrangement by Sylvia Woods

Lever harp players:
Set your sharping levers for the key signature, then set the low, middle and high A#s as shown above.
Sharping lever changes are indicated with diamond notes and also with octave wording.
Pedal changes are written below the bass staff.

Very slowly, and wistfully

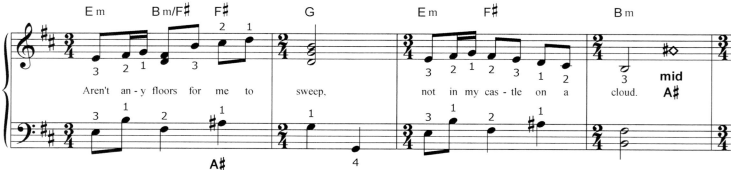

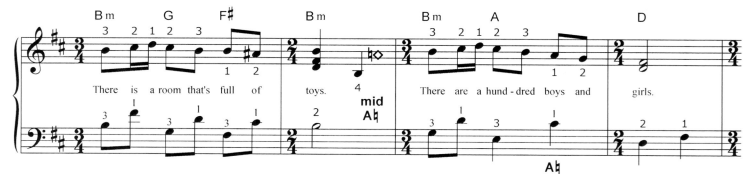

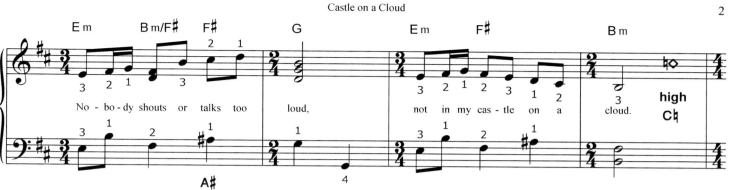

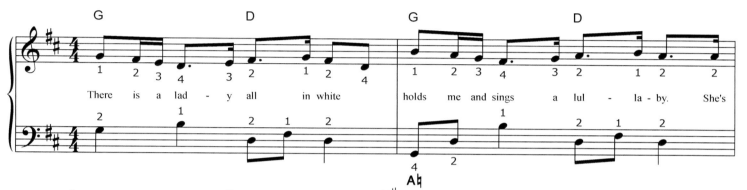

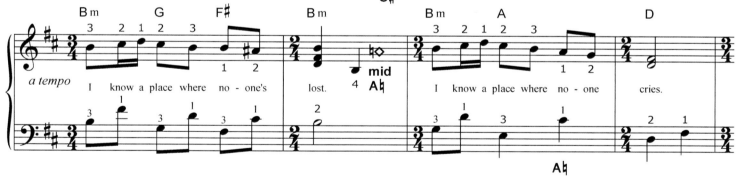

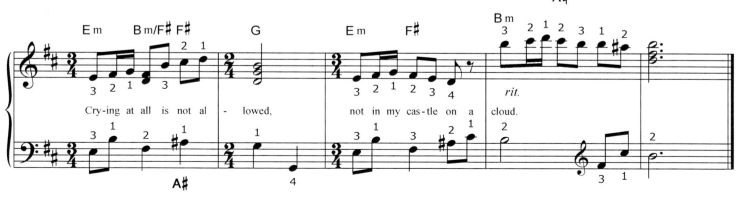

Castle on a Cloud
from *Les Misérables*
arrangement for lever harps tuned to flats, or pedal harps

Music by Claude-Michel Schönberg
Lyrics by Alain Boublil, Jean-Marc Natel
and Herbert Kretzmer
Harp arrangement by Sylvia Woods

Lever harp players:
Set your sharping levers for the key signature, then set the low, middle and high G#s as shown above.
Sharping lever changes are indicated with diamond notes and also with octave wording.
Pedal changes are written below the bass staff.

Very slowly, and wistfully

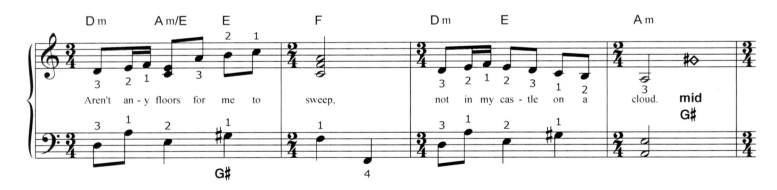

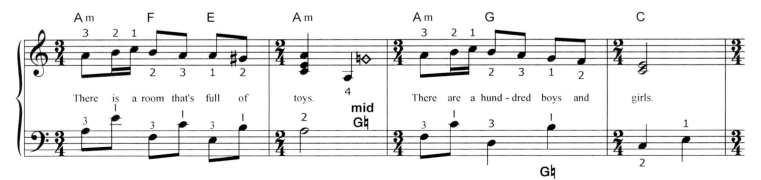

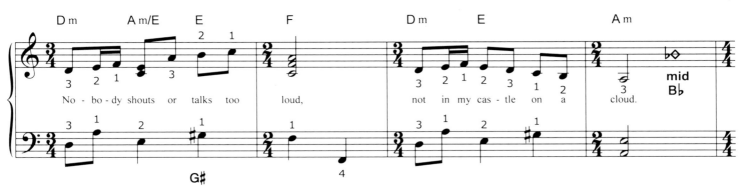

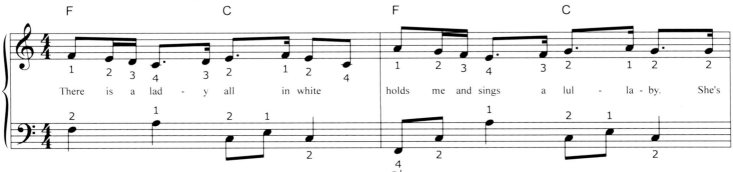

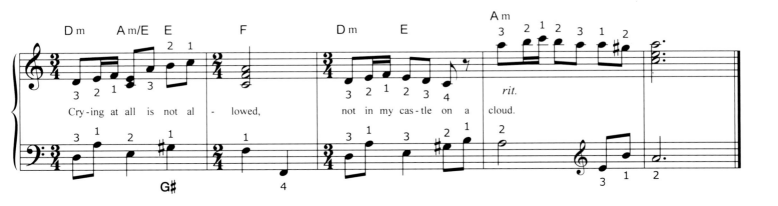

More Harp Arrangements of Pop Music
by Sylvia Woods

Beauty and the Beast

Music from Disney-Pixar's <u>Brave</u>

Bring Him Home from <u>Les Misérables</u>

Dead Poets Society

John Denver Love Songs

76 Disney Songs

Fireflies

Music from Disney <u>Frozen</u>

Groovy Songs of the 60s

Four Holiday Favorites

House at Pooh Corner / Return to Pooh Corner

Into the West from <u>The Lord of the Rings</u>

Lennon and McCartney

My Heart Will Go On from <u>Titanic</u>

Over the Rainbow from <u>The Wizard of Oz</u>

22 Romantic Songs

Safe & Sound

Stairway to Heaven

Music from Disney <u>Tangled</u>

Andrew Lloyd Webber Music

The Wizard of Oz

Theme from Disney-Pixar's <u>Up</u>

Available from harp music retailers and www.harpcenter.com

Sylvia Woods Harp Center
P.O. Box 223434, Princeville, HI 96722 U.S.A.

U.S. $7.95

888680 01258 8

HL00128725

ISBN 978-0-936661-63-6

9 780936 661636

Exclusively Distributed By

HAL•LEONARD®
CORPORATION
7777 W. BLUEMOUND RD. P.O. BOX 13819
MILWAUKEE, WISCONSIN 53213

With many thanks to Paul Baker

© 2014 by Sylvia Woods
Published by Woods Music & Books
P.O. Box 223434, Princeville, HI 96722, U.S.A.
www.harpcenter.com